GET UP & COMMIT

7 STEPS TO A HAPPY LIFE

KIRK TEACHOUT

IV QUARTER
PUBLISHING

CONTENTS

INTRODUCTION

A foundation is the most important piece of the home. Without a strong foundation, your home will eventually crack and break under the stress of storms. All of the concepts in this book are simple and, with intentional effort, you will be able to build and reinforce the strong foundation that you need to weather a lot of the storms that life has to throw at you.

Before flying on a plane, the stewardess will go through a series of instructions before takeoff that includes quickly buckling and unbuckling a seatbelt that no one will ever use and say, "if there should be a change in cabin pressure, put your mask on first before helping others". While I am NOT suggesting you wait until your life is in an emergency state because of stress levels, obesity, bankruptcy, etc. to do the action steps below, I AM suggesting that you focus on yourself for the next few months to get yourself in an optimal state to help others. When you succeed, you will be on your way to a more physical and emotional state of happiness which will be contagious and lead others to do the same.

We all have the same 24-hour day. The difference between where you are and where you want to be is what you do with them. You can commit 30 minutes or 1 hour a day to change your life.

WHAT TO EXPECT

As you go through each step, I will start with 3 important questions to reflect on before moving through the content of the action step. Whether you're reading or listening, I want you to sit down and really think hard about your answers and have them in the back of your mind. As you probably assumed, I will be touching on what I believe to be a good starting point to steer you in the right direction of success in this particular area of your life.

One thing I DO NOT want you to do is to go straight through this and try to change everything at once. Everyone is in a different place in life and if you try to change everything at once, you will be overwhelmed and quit. Ideally, I would like to see you read or listen through everything, take inventory of your life and implement one step as you feel comfortable. Make each of these a habit that you do not have to think about when you start the next action. It could be every week or every other week, but if things start to become too difficult, go back to what was going well and keep moving forward. Two steps forward and one step back is still progress.

Remember, these 7 steps are not the end all be all for these areas. Instead, they are springboards to action and guidance on where to start. The hardest part for most people is knowing where to start.

KEEPING YOUR PROMISES

I want to make a promise to you. I promise that you can do all of these steps, that you are enough, and that you can be happy with your life. No matter where you are in your life...whether a broke college student, just starting out in the real world, newly married, in the middle of your life, or retired and just looking for something to spice up your life...YOU CAN DO THIS!

Before you start implementing anything, you need to keep at least one small promise. If you are able to follow through, it will create a habit and help you with the bigger promises you are about to make.

Stop hitting the snooze button

Now, I want you to make this promise and write it down. Post it on your bathroom mirror so you see it every morning and every night. I WILL STOP HITTING THE SNOOZE BUTTON.

Take inventory of your life and after a couple of months, you will see that your life will be transformed. You will see yourself in the mirror, think back on who you were, and not recognize who started this journey. This does not mean that you will do these for the rest of your life perfectly. But it does mean that you will be on a good path to being a continual positive work in progress.

We are on this journey together, so let's get started!

CHAPTER 1
ROUTINE

Questions

1. *Do you have trouble sleeping?*
2. *How do you feel during the day? Chaotic? Tired? Stressed?*
3. *Do you feel that your brain is in a fog when you start your day?*

CHILDREN DO BEST WHEN THEY HAVE STABILITY AND A ROUTINE. For some reason, we lose the ability to recognize this as adults, but it is just as important now as it was when we were children.

Nighttime Routine

A nighttime routine gives you the ability to rest well, reset your mind, and rest your body. The problem is when your mind is racing, your thoughts are jumbled up, and you cannot seem to fall asleep. Plus, when you do fall asleep, you do not sleep well because your brain never seems to shut off throughout the night.

When you are not getting enough rest, it can create anxiety which will continue to add to your current stress level and increase the racing thoughts that you have at night. All of this process seems to be a never-ending cycle that cannot be broken, but there are a few different tricks and techniques to calm your brain and start a process to better sleep.

Henry Ford said, "Whether you think you can or think you can't, you are right." Your brain is the most powerful muscle in your body, so you need to train your brain about what to think and what to flush out before you lay down.

My favorite way to do this is by writing down a few things. Grab a notebook or a journal that can sit on your nightstand and use this as a tool to redirect your thoughts and get anything out of your mind that is not serving you for rest.

1. Write 3 positive things that happened during your day.

I want you to start with the positive, because if you do this, you will begin to naturally train your brain to always start with the positive things in life versus the negative.

2. Write 3 things that could have gone better today and how YOU could have changed the situation.

The serenity prayer from Alcoholics Anonymous has always fascinated me. "God, grant me the serenity to accept the things I cannot change, the courage to change the things I can, and the wisdom to know the difference." What could you have actually changed throughout your day? Think hard. If you have no control over it, do not worry about it. I want you to take ownership and responsibility for what has happened during your day instead of blaming others and, I know, this is easier said than done. Write down some of the things you could have changed and move on. A lot of times, our brains are stuck on a negative thought or situation that happened during the day that was not resolved. Regardless of how you feel, your brain will search for a resolution to these issues in your life. The problem will continue to stay in your mind until there is a solution. Write down 3 simple solutions.

3. Write down what needs to be done tomorrow and plan your day.

Once again, if you have priorities such as bills, emails, text messages, etc. that are not paid or responded to, your brain will continually think about a solution to solve these open-ended tasks. It's called the Zeigarnik Effect. It is the ability to remember interrupted or incomplete tasks over ones that are finished. One way to flush these from your brain is to write them down. It could be as simple as taking Billy to soccer practice at 3:30 pm and paying the electric bill. No matter how simple, write it down and flush the task from your mind to look at tomorrow.

Morning Routine

A great morning routine will almost always determine what kind of day you will have. If your alarm goes off and you hit the snooze button 3 times, you wake up 27 minutes late and rush to start your day. Not only will you be spending your day playing catch up, but you will also feel groggy or like your brain is in a fog because your alarm will wake you up towards the end of your final REM cycle or "deep sleep". When you hit the snooze button and go back to sleep, your brain sends you back into a REM cycle, but 9 minutes later, when that alarm goes off, you wake up in the middle of a REM cycle, which can throw your brain's internal clock off causing grogginess. We could go down a scientific rabbit hole as to why it is important not to hit the snooze button, but for now, I want you to just focus on how you feel when you wake up and how your day goes when you have a solid morning routine.

As much as I hate to say it, I feel better when I wake up a couple of hours before I need to get ready for the day and am mentally focused and more productive throughout the day. I am personally not a morning person, but I have come to love how I feel after my morning routine was developed.

To set up your morning routine, wake up at least an hour before you need to get your day started. If you cannot start doing it from day one, start by getting up 15 minutes earlier than you currently are for a few days and repeat that process until your morning routine can begin. What is important, though, are the things that you do with your time before you start your day.

1. Immediately get up, splash your face with cold water and brush your teeth.

You may not like it, but this will be the fastest way to get your mind and body awake for the day. Unless that is, you want to hop in a cold shower or a pool in your backyard if you have one. While brushing your teeth is an excellent hygiene practice, the cold water in your mouth as well as the quick, cold shock to your face increases the blood flow and your breathing due to a chemical called adrenaline. It is the adrenaline that will give you that quick burst of energy to wake up your whole body similar to caffeine without the side effects.

2. Exercise

I personally like to exercise in the morning before my day begins. It increases your blood flow and helps you feel productive, which will carry over into the rest of the day. Your activity needs to be something that will elevate your heart rate, like a brisk 20-30 minute walk around the neighborhood or going to the gym. It will feel uncomfortable at first but overtime it will become easier.

3. Sit down and prepare for your day.

Does a leader go into battle without knowing all of the details of the battle? Not a wise one! When someone else's life is at stake, you would hope that the leader has done everything possible to win the battle. Right? Do you think it is wise to go throughout your day unprepared? You are the leader of your life and your life is at stake.

Remember that notebook or journal that you planned your day out with the night before? Take a look at it, and see what you want to adjust. If there are some hard tasks or situations ahead, write down a few positives for them and stand prepared. When you are prepared for your day, you can be more productive and ready to conquer it.

What is cool about waking up an hour before you need to start your day is that you will most likely be ready for your nighttime routine because you will have squeezed every ounce of productivity. At this time, you will be tired and ready to rest which will allow your brain and body to rest better. Your productivity will increase if you get better rest and will allow your morning routine to be easier the next day.

Now, doing this every day at the start is not going to be easy. But you can do it!

Do you want better sleep? Do you want your day to be less chaotic and have more energy? Create great nighttime and morning routines and stick to them!

ACTION STEPS

- Get a Journal/Notebook
- Write down 3 positive things that happened during the day.
- Write down 3 things that could have gone better today and how YOU could have changed the situation.
- Write down what needs to be done tomorrow and plan your day.
- Set your alarm at least an hour before your day starts
- Brush your teeth and splash cold water on your face
- Exercise
- Sit down and prepare for your day

CHAPTER 2
EXERCISE

Questions

1. *Do you have a positive hobby?*
2. *Do you have a positive body image?*
3. *Do you have frequent periods of stress?*

YES, I KNOW, I'M GOING TO TELL YOU THAT YOU NEED TO exercise. But, that is because it is SUPER beneficial to not only your physical health but your mental health as well!

The most obvious one is the help to manage your weight. Whether you are trying to lose weight or gain weight, exercise is one of the ways to do both. Here is a list of benefits that exercise has for your life:

- Weight Management

- Heart Disease & Stroke Prevention

- Diabetes Type 2 & Metabolic Syndrome Prevention

- Strengthening of Your Bones & Muscles

- Manage Chronic Conditions

- Stress Reducer

There are many other added benefits to exercise, which is why it is extremely important. Studies show that even an extra 10 minutes of exercise a day would make a difference to your overall health. I want to take it a step further and say you should at least exercise 20-30 minutes a day. Whether that is in the morning, as I suggested in the previous chapter, or at night is your choice.

If you are exercising on a regular basis, great! There are still ways that you can improve what you are doing. For now, I am going to give you a few ways you can start the process and assess where you are physically.

Simple Physical Assessment

1. Check your pulse before and after you walk 1 mile.

Was it difficult? Were you out of breath? Could you walk twice that amount?

- Write down your pulse before and after and a description of how that felt.

2. How long does it take you to walk that mile?

- Write down your time.

3. How many push-ups can you do? Do you need to do a push-up on your knees?

- Write down how many you can do in one sitting.

4. Sit down on the floor with your legs in front of you and stretch forward to try and touch your toes. Can you get halfway? Can you go all the way and touch your toes?

- Write down how far you can get.

5. Get a "soft" tape measure or a body tape measure from your local store or online and measure around your waist right above the hips.

- Write down the measurement.

6. Stand on a scale and weigh yourself.

- Write down the weight

As you start with your exercise or increase your current plan, make sure to start the increase of activity slowly. If you jump the gun and do too much, too fast, you will end up quitting. Start slowly so you can create the discipline that you need to continually increase your exercise type or time.

Make sure to listen to your body. While raising funds for a charity by cycling a mile per dollar, I noticed some pain in my left hip. I knew that if I attempted to keep riding the miles I would end up doing more damage to my body. Instead, I decided to take a couple of days off, stretched, and felt just fine. You need to listen to what your body is telling you. I'm not saying that you should quit because you may be a little out of breath. Pushing your body a little is how we get stronger. I am, however, telling you that you need to know if something could go wrong and be honest with yourself.

Lastly, an athlete such as yourself needs to stretch before and after the exercise. If you have flexibility in your muscles, you lower the risk of injury.

Now, again, take the notebook that you planned your day with and write all of these numbers and descriptions down. As you go through the next few weeks and are writing down your improvements, you will notice a difference in your numbers. That is PROGRESS!

Do you want a positive hobby? Do you want a positive body image? Do you want to reduce stress?

Simple Exercises

Walk 5,000 to 10,000 steps daily.

25 Jumping Jacks

15 Squats

30 Second Plank

10 Lunges Per Side

10 Push Ups

30 Seconds of Running In Place - High Knees

10 Sit Ups

20 Crunches

ACTION STEPS

- Use your journal/notebook to write down assessment notes
- When you are planning your day, write down what exercises you will do
- Write the time and amount of exercise you completed each day

CHAPTER 3
DIET/NUTRITION

Questions

1. *Do you have a lack of energy?*
2. *How do you feel after eating? Bloated? Swollen? Sluggish?*
3. *Do you exercise but can't seem to lose that extra 5 pounds?*

IF YOU HAVE EVER MADE A NEW YEARS RESOLUTION LIKE I HAVE, where you eat nothing but chicken, nuts, vegetables, and salads for the first 3 weeks and tell everyone you feel great because you did, you will know what I am talking about in this chapter. For those that made a new years resolution to eat better tomorrow and are still waiting until tomorrow, I also know how you feel and I hope to enlighten you in this chapter.

Your diet and nutrition make up a large portion of the

outcome of your life. Doctors are now coining the phrase, Diabetes Type 3 for Alzheimer's patients because it is largely due to a patient's diet and nutrition. So, controlling your diet is a VERY important part of your life, but through the self-control and discipline that you are developing right now, you can do it!

A good rule of thumb is called the 80/20 rule. 80% of the time, you need to eat a balanced, nutritious diet so you can maintain a healthy lifestyle. 20% percent of the time, you can cheat a little, but not in excess, because if you're doing it right, it will make you feel terrible. Even professional athletes have some crazy french toast smothered in peanut butter on cheat days.

To me, the hardest part of figuring out what was right was portion control. I was raised in the south where you have 5 sides to every meal, in addition to some sort of bread and a pound of sugar in your sweet tea. With that being said, I have learned to balance my diet more by simplifying what is on my plate.

- 3 oz high-fat protein (Salmon, Eggs) or 4 oz low-fat protein (Chicken, Sirloin, Lean Beef)

- 1 large handful of vegetables

- 6 oz lightly seasoned brown rice/red potatoes/sweet potatoes

NOW THIS VARIES SOMETIMES DEPENDING ON IF I AM TRAINING for something or if I want to trim off a few pounds. You can go with that structure literally or there are a million combinations to go with this simple setup, such as these:

Seasoned Chicken, Asparagus, Red Potatoes

Sausage, Brussel Sprouts, Sweet Potatoes

Chicken Tacos in a Bowl (Seasoned Chicken, Rice, Black Beans, Onions, Pico, Cheese)

Egg Roll in a Bowl (Cabbage or Cole Slaw Mix, Sausage, Egg, Sliced Green Onions)

Campfire Meals (Beef, Carrots, Squash, Brocolli, Corn on the Cob, Red Potatoes)

AGAIN, YOUR DIET IS SUPER IMPORTANT. IF YOU WANT MORE energy in your day, you will need to control your diet more. Why? Because you are what you eat, and it is a fact that food with calories gives you energy. However, when you eat fatty foods, it increases the production of serotonin in your system, which can make you feel sluggish and regulates your attention and behavior. No wonder my kids wreck the house when they are hyped up on sugar and fatty foods.

Simple Starters to Cut Out of Your Diet

- Sugary Drinks (Sodas, Sweet Tea, etc.)

- French Fries

- Chips

- White Bread

- Candy

- Ice Cream

- Alcohol

Common Objection: I cannot afford healthy meals.

This is not true. Yes, the healthy options are more expensive the more organic, farm-raised, free-range you go. However, there are ways to still be healthy and have a balanced diet. If you look online for healthy meals on a budget, there will be more meals than you can cook or put together that are available on a lower budget.

Do you want to have more energy during the day? Do you want to feel less bloated and sluggish? Do you want to lose those 5 extra pounds?

ACTION STEPS

- Go through your cabinets and clean out some of the food you do not need. Maybe use some of them for a cheat day instead of throwing them away.
- Create a list of things that you can cut out of your diet and stick to it.
- Create a list of 5-10 meals that are healthier that you would enjoy and rotate them.
- Create a list of not-so-terrible cheat meals to look forward to once a week or so.

CHAPTER 4
BUDGET

Questions

1. *If you did not get your next paycheck, would you be able to pay the bills?*
2. *Do you want to save more money?*
3. *Do you want to survive, or thrive?*

THE DAY AND AGE OF ELECTRONIC PAYMENTS VS CASH, CREDIT VS debit cards, and this budget style or no budget style have come into our lives in some form or fashion. 63% of Americans spend all that they make, saving very little, if any, and are one paycheck away from total financial destruction. THIS DOES NOT HAVE TO BE YOU!

Let's get back to the basics! Sit down and do an assessment of how much money you are bringing home and how much you are spending on a monthly basis. This may sound weird, but you will likely be spending more than you realize.

Get your bank and credit card statements for one month and highlight every time money is deposited into your account. Everything else is an expense or part of what you spent throughout the past month. Create 3 different sections on a sheet of paper or on your computer that are labeled: Income, Bills, Extras

As you are writing all of these categories down, be honest with yourself as to what is an extra. You may love that subscription service, but is it a necessity in your life? I do this exercise at least twice a year because we tend to add small subscriptions and monthly payments without thinking about them compounding and adding a lot to our monthly expenses.

After you have completed your assessment, you need to get your thinking right before moving money around and canceling things.

I do not believe that there is a specific plan out there that you and your relatives can all use and produce the same outcome. I do believe that there are some guiding principles that will allow everyone to be good stewards of their money. First, with short term thinking in mind to survive but, second, with long term thinking to determine what you do overall and thrive.

SHORT TERM THINKING

Become someone who saves instead of someone who spends. Something that I started doing to combat my spending was to ask if I needed this current item to live or make money. If I did not need it, I quickly stopped and transferred the amount I was about to spend on that item to my savings account. Your spending is more important than how much money you make. There are very successful people that make a lot of money but still live paycheck to paycheck because they spend every dime they bring in. Get your spending under control.

Long Term Thinking

What do you need to live comfortably for 20+ years in retirement? There are a lot of complex and complicated formulas to figure out this number, but it is also based on how you want to live in retirement. Take your current spending and multiply it by 25. Once you get your spending under control, reassess and see what you would like to spend in retirement. $30,000 a year in spending x 25 = $750,000

Remember, you will hopefully have put a plan in place to pay off most if not all of your debts and should not need as much to spend in retirement.

Guiding Principles

1. Rainy Day Fund

How long could you survive if you did not have money coming in? 6 months? 1 month? 2 weeks?

Most experts say that you need to have at least 3 - 6 months' worth of your income for large emergencies. Take your monthly expenses and multiply them by 3 - 6 and write down the amount and stick it on your mirror. SAVE THIS FIRST!

2. Debt Stacking

Write down all of the minimum payment amounts for your debt. Hopefully, you have gone through and cleaned up some subscriptions that you do not use and have freed up some funds that you can put toward your debt. If you freed up $50, add it on top of your lowest balance of the debt. Once that balance is paid off, apply that payment to the next lowest balance, and so on.

Let's say you have a $100 payment on car #1 and a balance of $1000 and another $100 payment on car #2 with a balance of $1500. Currently, it will take you 10 months to pay off car #1 and 15 months to pay off car #2, by making the minimum monthly payment. What is cool about debt stacking is this next process. Car #1 has been paid off after 10 months and car #2 still has 5 months left out of the 15 total months. You are used to paying $100 a month for car #1, so do not say, "WAHOO, I HAVE $100 EXTRA TO SPEND!". Since you are not missing the $100 and are used to spending it, put that towards the payment for car #2. Now, you are putting $200 a month into car #2, which will pay it off in a little over 2 months. Instead of taking 15 months total to pay both of the cars off, it only took you 13 months with the same amount of money.

If you add the extra $50 that you freed up from your wise budgeting to the lower balance of car #1, you will pay off car #1 faster. Now, instead of paying off car #1 in 10 months, you will be able to pay it off in 7 months. Take that $250 from the payment of car #1 and car #2 and pay off both cars in 10 months instead of 15 months.

	Car #1			Car #2		
	Balance	$	1,000.00	Balance	$	1,500.00
	Minimum Payment	$	100.00	Minimum Payment	$	100.00
	Interest Rate		0.0%	Interest Rate		0.0%
Month	Payment		Balance	Payment		Balance
1	$	150.00	$ 850.00	$	100.00	$ 1,400.00
2	$	150.00	$ 700.00	$	100.00	$ 1,300.00
3	$	150.00	$ 550.00	$	100.00	$ 1,200.00
4	$	150.00	$ 400.00	$	100.00	$ 1,100.00
5	$	150.00	$ 250.00	$	100.00	$ 1,000.00
6	$	150.00	$ 100.00	$	100.00	$ 900.00
7	$	100.00	$ -	$	150.00	$ 750.00
8	$	-	$ -	$	250.00	$ 500.00
9	$	-	$ -	$	250.00	$ 250.00
10	$	-	$ -	$	250.00	$ -

3. Invest the Difference

Invest a percentage of your income to grow your long-term financial freedom account. Once you have hit your target number for your rainy day fund and put aside some extra money to put into your debt payments, invest the difference between what you have left and what you were saving. I do suggest reaching out to an expert in this field before investing your money in anything specific.

4. Education

As Warren Buffet once said, "The greatest investment you can make is an investment in yourself. The more you learn, the more you'll earn." You need to continually invest in education, such as books, podcasts, seminars, events, etc. You will never see a greater return in anything else other than yourself.

5. Play Money

This principle is going to feel odd when you are trying to save and hit goals, but it is just as important. You need to set a small percentage aside for you to spend on yourself. It can be any type of reward for your hard work or something relaxing. You need to spend this money and feel good about it so you do not get burned out and not enjoy life.

Here is a good balance to where you can be placing your money. If you want to figure out the percentage you are spending, add up the amount in each of these categories and divide them by the amount of income you bring home.

55% - ESSENTIALS (FOOD, GAS, BILLS)

10% - Long-Term Saving (Rainy Day Fund, Vacations, etc)

10% - Education (Mentorship, Books, etc.)

10% - Financial Freedom Account (Investments, Retirement, etc)

5-10% - Giving (Charities, Church, etc)

5-10% - Play Money (SPEND ON YOURSELF)

Now that you have all of these tools, sit down and get to work. Set aside a couple of times a year to do this and audit your budget. Once you get this budget machine running, you will not just survive, YOU WILL THRIVE!

Do you want to stop living paycheck to paycheck? Do you want to save more money? Do you want to thrive financially?

ACTION STEPS

- Get your bank and credit card statements and see where your money is going
- Be honest with yourself
- Get rid of all of the unnecessary expenses
- Create a mindset to spend less, not make more.
- Create a plan to get your rainy day fund built up
- Assign an extra dollar amount to your lowest debt balance
- Reach out to a financial advisor to start investing
- Invest in yourself
- Spend a small percentage of money on yourself to reward yourself
- Get your spending percentages as balanced as you can

CHAPTER 5
TIME MANAGEMENT

Questions

1. *Do you feel you could do more with your day?*
2. *Do you feel there are not enough hours in the day?*
3. *Do you find yourself being interrupted while working?*

As I said at the beginning, we all have the same 24-hour day. The difference between where you are and where you want to be is how you manage your time throughout the day. If you have a job, you probably have a schedule of the work that needs to get done throughout the day. Businesses are created this way to allow their teams to be more productive and efficient as well as reduce the stress level around the office.

1. WRITE DOWN YOUR TASKS

Look at the tasks that you wrote down in your morning routine and see if there are any other tasks that need to be added. Divide any larger tasks into smaller ones to help you focus.

2. Prioritize Tasks

I like to rate my tasks from 1 to 3. 1 being top priority tasks that need to be finished today, 2 being moderate tasks that should be finished today, and 3 being tasks that can be finished today but will be ok to push to tomorrow.

3. Parkinson's Law

"Work expands so as to fill the time available for its completion." The best illustration for this would be in school. You had a paper you needed to write and you had several months until the deadline. For some reason, you decide to wait until the night or two before and somehow finish the paper just in time. You did not need the full months to complete this task, you only needed one or two days. When you have 6 hours for a task, you will fill that time even if it should only take you an hour.

If you want to get faster and more productive, get a timer and set it right in front of you. I used to set a timer for an hour in front of me while I was mixing music and I got way more finished than if it was not set. Normally, mixing music would take me hours. After a while, I learned to be more efficient and strategic with my decisions to finishing everything in that hour.

4. Write Down A Schedule

Get a piece of paper or a calendar and start with your morning routine. Work your way down through your day, adding your tasks until your nighttime routine.

5. Get Rid of Distractions

There are a couple of things you should do. First, go through your phone and turn off all of the notifications on your apps that are not necessary. Once again, you need to be honest with yourself because they say that it takes an average of 23 minutes and 15 seconds to get focused again if you are interrupted during your day. After you have turned off your notifications, put your phone away while you are focused on work.

ARE YOU GOING TO DO MORE WITH YOUR DAY? DO YOU HAVE more than enough hours in the day? Will you be honest and respect your own time?

ACTION STEPS

- Get a calendar and a timer that is NOT on your phone
- Create your ideal schedule to accomplish tasks
- Get rid of distractions

CHAPTER 6
FIND A MENTOR

Questions

1. *Do your friends build you up, or pull you down?*
2. *Are the people around you supportive of your goals and dreams?*
3. *Do you find yourself quitting too quickly?*

JIM ROHN SAID,

> "you're the average of the five people you spend the most time with" and "show me your friends and I'll show you your future"

Does that mean that you are only influenced by the closest 5 people to you? No, but the closest people that you interact with and listen to the most will determine your trajectory in life.

I am not telling you to completely abandon your family. I am saying that you need to limit your interactions with negative and unsupportive family members and set boundaries. Enjoy the quality time together but once negativity starts to come into the conversation, politely explain why you do not want to speak in this way.

The great thing about mentorship these days is that you have access to almost anyone for free. Sure, you can spend thousands of dollars going to events and purchasing courses that great people have, and they are beneficial. But, you know, you are able to listen to podcasts, read books, and pull out many other forms of content for free. I have a close inner circle of people I listen to in person, but I like to think of that 5th person in my inner circle as whatever book or podcast I'm listening to at the time.

Another great way to get mentorship is by taking people to lunch or coffee. Most successful people will be more than willing to let you take them to lunch or coffee and share the information they have spent their life acquiring. If you are able to hire a coach or mentor, great! If not, you have no excuses. You can find it if you want it badly enough!

Life is a journey and so is being mentored. Make sure to do this on a consistent basis. If you have a commute to work, are you listening to music or the news? Use this time to listen to an audiobook or a podcast. Do you work from home? Set aside 30 minutes a day to sit and read, listen to an audiobook or watch a good YouTube video from your favorite mentors. My wife and I will sometimes sit down and listen to our favorite podcasts right before we get ready for bed as part of our nighttime routine.

Do you want friends that build you up? Do you want supportive people to help you with your goals and dreams?

ACTION STEPS

- Write down the 5 closest people to you and rate them on a scale of 1-10 for being supportive and then being encouraging.
- Assess whether you should find different friends.
- Block off time during your day to read, listen, or watch 30 minutes of inspirational and self-improvement material.
- Write down 3-5 people you would like to take to lunch or coffee to learn from.
- Be consistent

CHAPTER 7
SERVE OTHERS

Questions

1. *When you approach people, do you only talk about yourself?*
2. *When you end a conversation, where do you leave it?*
3. *Are you looking to be more successful?*

NOW THAT YOU HAVE BEEN WORKING ON YOURSELF AND HAVE developed your discipline, it's time to give back. John F. Kennedy said, "ask not what your country can do for you – ask what you can do for your country" during his inaugural address to get Americans to contribute in some way to public service. How do you approach life?

Early on in my young adult life, I remember constantly trying to figure out how "I" was going to be successful...trying to figure out how "I" was going to make more money...what "I" was going to do to get there. After going through school and starting my first business, it always seemed to be difficult to really get off the ground. That is until I joined a business group that met once a week to discuss each other's businesses for 12 weeks straight.

Before the meetings began, the group leader gave us all 2 books, "The Pumpkin Plan" and "The Go-Giver". I read both but "The Go-Giver" was able to put into words what I was trying to figure out for a long time. After the 12-week sessions, I continued to work with a couple of the people in the group and started to shift my mindset. Instead of how can I make more money, I started asking questions like, how can I get more people full-time in the work that they love? Throughout the next 4 years, my company exploded to heights I had never seen before. That change came from a decision I made after reading one book and turning my focus from myself to serving others.

When you shift your thinking from what serves you to serving others, everyone wins. The people around you win because they have a friend, a companion, or an unlikely stranger who was able to help in a time of need. You win because greater things happen in your life when you are not focused on yourself. Sure, we are all selfish, but when you are serving others out of the goodness of your heart, you will see true change in yourself and others. As Jesper says in one of my favorite Christmas movies, Klaus, "A true selfless act always sparks another."

Ask different questions at the beginning and end of a conversation. Genuinely ask how people are doing today and empathize with them. If they are having a good day, have joy with them. If they are having a bad day, you get the opportunity to make their day better. At the end of the conversation, genuinely ask if there is anything you can do for them. You would be surprised at how touching this question is and a lot of people have no idea how to answer it because no one asks them.

ARE YOU GOING TO STOP TALKING ABOUT YOURSELF AND BE interested in others? Will you switch your focus from how can I be more successful to how can I help others be more successful?

ACTION STEPS

- Think about where you are in life and where you have the opportunity to serve others.
- Start being intentional in your conversations with your family, friends, and strangers at the beginning and the end.

GO TIME!

My personal timeline to reinforce new tasks and start to build new habits is anywhere from 2-3 weeks. This is just the time that it takes my mind and body to get over the hump of dread. I take on one or two tasks at a time, get over the hump, and move on to the next task. This allows me to put my full focus on what needs to happen in a couple of tasks versus dividing my efforts all at once.

There are studies that show the average person takes around 2-8 months to create a habit that becomes automatic. This is primarily why gym memberships start to fall off at the end of January and February each year. As you take baby steps, you will create more and more discipline in yourself. I tell you this not to discourage you, but to empower you and tell you that anything worth anything takes work and consistency.

GO TIME!

Are you happy where you are in life or do you know it could be better? All you have to do is get up and commit.

If you appreciate the information in this book, I would love it if you could leave a 5-star review and your feedback!

Printed in Great Britain
by Amazon

32928017R00030